Kiss the Rushing Day Goodbye

Sue Amanda Carter

Kiss the Rushing Day Goodbye

Dedication

For my daughter Lucy. Thank you for getting me to
where I am today and for always sticking by my side.

I want to thank my friends, including my boyfriend Dean,
and Helen and Phil, who have been there for me.
I want to thank my family, especially my mum and dad.
I would like to thank Jude Aquilina, my editor and mentor,
and Kylie Harrison, my peer worker,
and all Life Without Barriers staff past and present:
Zel, Kerri, Daphne and Jodie.
There are too many people to thank.

Kiss the Rushing Day Goodbye
ISBN 978 1 76041 379 8
Copyright © Sue Amanda Carter 2017

First published 2017 by
GINNINDERRA PRESS
PO Box 3461 Port Adelaide 5015 Australia
www.ginninderrapress.com.au

Contents

Foreword	7
Introduction	9
Nature's Supreme Simplicity	**11**
The Countryside	13
The Sun Shines	14
Fire and Ice, Rats and Mice	15
Morning	16
For Me	17
Each Day Anew	18
Late at Night	19
Spiritual Musings	**21**
Moonwash	23
Action	24
Human	25
Dreamworld	26
Dream Reading	27
Seeds of Creativity	**29**
Tonight	31
Movies	32
Praiseworthy Pursuits	33
Friends and Family	**35**
A Problem	37
The Butterfly and the Caterpillar	38
Unravelling	39
The Draw	40
Silver Strings of Mental Health	**41**
Hellhole	43
Nurturing the Taproot	44

Just Resorts	45
Heaven in Hell	46
Eye of the Storm	47
I Must Walk in a Straight Line	48

Love's Healing Grace   49

Love	51
Forget Being a Princess	52
Living on the Line	53
Barnacles	54
Relationship Breakdown	55
Role Play	56

Life on Earth   59

Fruit and Vegetables	61
This Life…	62
Acting on Life's Big Stage	63
Ticking	64

Freedom's Key   65

Let Me be Free to be Me	67
Keep Looking	68
Hard to be Alone and Happy	69
Free?	70
I Need Some Polish	71
The Human Soup	72

About the Author   73

Foreword

Sue Amanda Carter. Where on earth do I start? My mum. My friend. My confidante. My confusion. My sparkle amidst the rough. My hero amongst the ups and downs. Believe me, I could have bought a house by now, with the amount I've helped out. But would I change it for the world? No. There is beauty found in the abstract. And Sue is definitely that. Mum's journey is the stuff movies are made of: a timeless odyssey of joy, pain, illness, loss, hope, heartache, opportunity and disappointment… Much like the (soon to be) nine billion other stories out there. Each with its own tapestry of life's crazy stories, each unique.

Sometimes I think we are all suffering the same condition really – LIFE! And it's precisely how this most curious conundrum deals you its fateful cards that determine much of the outcome. I often feel like I am the mother…but then, she so easily puts me back in my place by being SO right about almost everything. Being young and an Aries, I naturally think that I know it all, but more often than not I realise Mum knows it all. Constantly going over all her findings from this life…madly scribbling away to beat life's ticking clock, she gets her poetry down on paper.

I hope you enjoy Mum's ponderings: the cutting truth, her whimsical curiosity, her illness and despair, her joy, ramblings and epiphanies. This is HER truth. So what is yours? Let creativity show you. Sometimes as humans, our creativity is the only thing that brings light to the darkness.

Lucy Bayet

PS. I would like to take the opportunity to express my deepest thanks and appreciation to all of the services our country has and the beautiful people behind them who are there for those, when family is not. To Life without Barriers and other organisations and people, to those who offer help where others don't seem to bother, who become a friend when people need one the most. The carers who often go unappreciated and the workers who open their hearts and listen to those unheard stories. May life be a mirror of your kindness and good karma reward your efforts. Here's to YOU. Keep shining your light and let nothing put it out.

Introduction

In a confusing world of double standards, mixed emotions, contradicting examples and hypocrisy, it is no wonder the younger generation has grown restless, rebellious and impatient for answers. People are living freer and seemingly happier lives, but for this new freedom and endless boundaries a high price must be paid.

Upon my travels, I have learned many things and have been confronted with bundles of opinions and ideas that have thus broadened my mind. I have fathomed through the garbage and persuasions, and am thankful that my childish ideals and attitudes have not changed to any great extent.

I would love to change and challenge the world via many outlets but as a human being I would never be able to beat some of the destructive systems and bodies confronting us today. I cannot make any direct attacks on the powerful and sometimes dishonest money machines that run the world; so I must accept defeat and pray that one day things will change positively and for the benefit of the majority.

When I am not dwelling on the sad or bad, despite infuriating occurrences against man and nature, I am generally a very happy, content person, my personal theme being the three big Ls: Love, Light and Laughter. By the age of twenty-one I'd had many rich and wonderful experiences, and I believed that I had 'sorted myself out'. Many questions will always remain unanswered, but I must not dwell on this, as life is too short. I love life and the things it has to offer. I lead a simple life and try not to confuse my humble existence with complex analysis.

Life is simple and I strongly believe the most worthwhile

things in life are free. An emotional person with a passionate love for nature, a keen sense of adventure and a zest for life, living most of the time in a self-confessed dream world, I have recorded impressions of a few of my thoughts and reactions to life around me.

Sue Carter

Nature's Supreme Simplicity

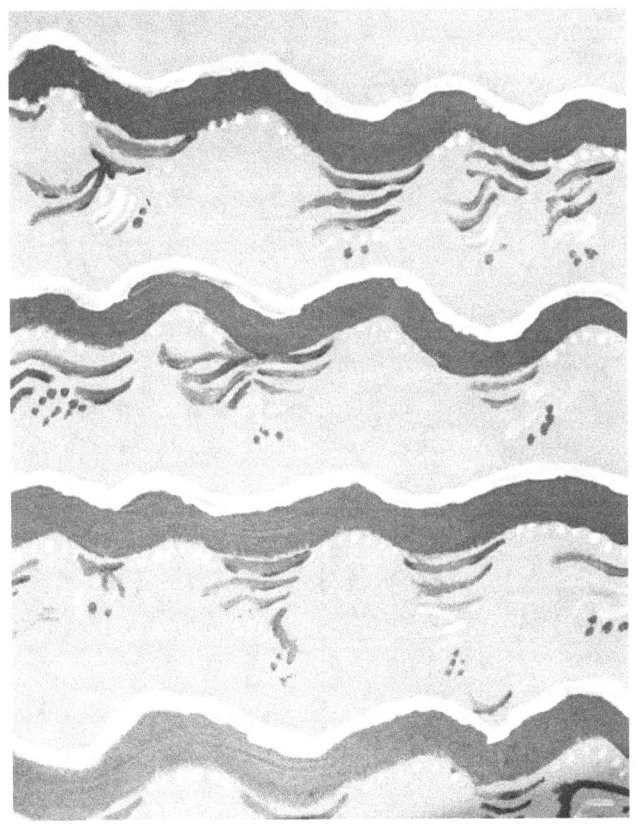

The Countryside

The countryside,
green and fresh
whispers innocence
teases my sensitivity
flows with me through time.

I bathe in the elements
growing wild and free.
Man may destroy
but will never conquer
our innate naturalness.

The Sun Shines

The sun shines
the birds sing bright
this afternoon brings
a quiet time
time to think
time to relax
to reflect on days
on friends and seasons
that flickered by.

I can hear my own heartbeat.
I can hear myself breathe.
Birds are singing
and we are talking
in between silver slivers
of sacred silence.

Fire and Ice, Rats and Mice

Man has always destroyed nature.
Nature's had enough. Nature's transitory nature
reclaims the heavens, proclaims her forces
will conquer. And nature always wins.
The war has only just begun. Man progresses
from mere nuisance taking a free ride,
to the unspoken – another wave, another trough
in the battle between economy and nature's law.
And who really wins?

Morning

Morning has come, but
once again
there's a million things to do…
an accepted fact
that will eternally remain.
When chores are done,
outside duties wrapped up,
I rush into town
and scurry around…
I must not let the troops down.

My mission completed
but few thing done.
I am not defeated,
I'm still on the run.
The day's light dims
so I stop for a minute
draw a deep breath
and with a sigh
I kiss the rushing day
goodbye
and hurry home.

For Me

Life I want,
where do you wait?
What shall we do?
When do we sail
upon that sea
so you and me
can just
be?

On land
the masses
wail
for the felling of trees
I hope seas of trees
will still stand tall
when all else fails.

Each Day Anew

Oh, the heaven in dawn
each new day
comes but once
in a lifetime.

Winter breeze
circulating Antarctic chills
over diamond hills.
Mount Lofty calls
with whispers of cold winds
blowing and swirling.

Refreshed, revitalised
my eyes open wide.
I pause again
in this long line
of sunrises.

Late at Night

Late at night
the lights are dim.
This is where
life begins.
In the security of the night
in the cover of darkness
in a corner of thought
and life analysed
great thoughts
clouds of feelings
of heavy dealings
of life, awheelin'
buzzing through my brain.

A million electrodes
cosmic waves
devious thoughts
plans for tomorrow
flash and spark.
Then all is sombre
all is dull
but through this blackness
beams a ray.
A little laser of sunshine?
A little taste of moonshine?
No – just a man-made instrument
to suffocate darkness
to infuriate nature
to pacify hunger.

Man rides the waves of an ocean
tosses the coin, flips the lid,
flicks a switch.
Nature eventually wins.
It's winning now –
changes of season
loss of reason,
little rays of hope
in the streetlight.

Spiritual Musings

Moonwash

I'm having a moon bath.
There's a sea of desert stars
in the midnight sky.
I'm having a moon bath
feeling energised –
a powerful battery
a huge quartz crystal.

I'm having a moon bath
thinking of my daughter
her glowing smile.
I'm happy in this night
with no end.
The sun
is too fierce
and keeps kicking me.

I'm having a moon bath
washing bright horrors away.

Action

Kiss a dying flower
and pray it grows again,
it might choose life for you.
Order it to live
and it will surely die.
Human communication
is often absurd.
So many words are breaths
of air wasted.
So, physically do something.
Speak after your actions
and you will have truth.
Acting after speaking
may reduce you to a liar.
Actions take you higher.

Human

I want to live
I want to give
and forgive.
I want to accept you
I want to love you.
I say I will
I say I can
I say I should do this
I say I should do that.
I want to save a soul
I want to feed the hungry
I want to stop a war.
I am happy
I am also a hypocrite
unknowingly.
I am sorry.
A harsh word, I know –
I must accept that
we are all hypocrites
because we are human
but we want to live
we want to give.

Dreamworld

Yes, I do live in a dream world.
My dreams rarely turn into reality
but at least I have dreams.
People can rob me of everything I own
degrade me, accuse me, misinterpret me
but I can tune out from harsh reality
and sink into my invisible world,
act as I want, be who I want, say what I want.

A mild form of insanity:
an uncontrollable urge to travel
in my mind; to achieve, to laugh, to sing.
In my dreams I can dance and dive.
There is nothing wrong with dreaming.
The more dreaming you have
the more hope you generate, the greater the desire
the more chances you have
of a dream coming true.
Dream, dream, don't give up,
the laws of probability are on your side.

Dream Reading

for Lucy

Dreams are freedom.
I love to dream
of you and me
of this and that.

I love to dream
of fantasy in the skies
of escaping into the wild.

I am thankful
for the knowledge
some dreams
bring me. Gifts,
like you – proof
that some dreams
do come true.

Seeds of Creativity

Tonight

Tonight I just
sit and ponder…

what fun it is to
wonder
 wonder
  wonder.

Movies

I saw a movie today.
It took my breath away.
Thank you writers
and actors and a thousand others
who make movies
that reflect myself,
my attitudes,
my dreams –
these stories excite me.
And my heart beams
brighter for a while
life offers more
than it seems
when I recall
the scenes.

Praiseworthy Pursuits

There are many
such treasures
unwrapped
like stolen kisses
gentle
whispers.

Not always sex
just gentle
human touch
gentle
whispers.

No winners.
No losers.
We all try hard
to earn love's
gentle
whispers.

Friends and Family

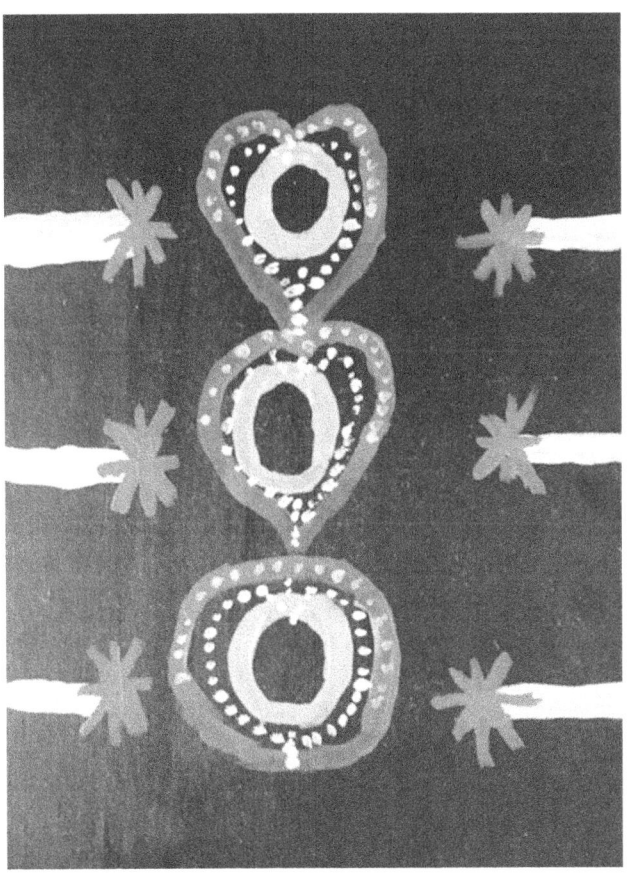

A Problem

I was feeling down, dirt low,
when my greatest companion
said to me, 'Come on, babe.
What's your problem? Communicate.'
And I learned what lovely threads
relationships are spun with.

And I did just that,
I opened up
my emotions ran wild
through laughter
tears, hours, but my companion
did not give up. He listened
and he listened and that is why
I love him.

The Butterfly and the Caterpillar

for my daughter Lucy

Lucy is the butterfly
who flutters by me.
I am the caterpillar.
Life together
is sunnier, sillier
even if only one of us
can fly.
Rare as rainbows
lovely as dew
I am grateful
for the miracle
that is you.

Make my glass
half full
I'd drink the brew
of truth for you.
I'd climb
forsaken mountains
and cling to shifting pebbles
of hope, just to know
that you, Lucy
will return and renew.

Unravelling

People
same ingredients
different packaging.

The Draw

There are no such things
as winners or losers
we are all victims
of circumstance, of genes, of parents
and the environment we stumble in to.

I married a poor, broken
mentally ill man
driven by hatred;
and he hurt me irreparably.
He thought he was Jesus Christ
and tried to nail my soul
to his darkness.

But life is a miracle
and worth working on.
There's almost seven billion people
on earth, all thinking differently.
My sisters and my brothers
all contain light, love and warmth,
yet blame and shame
threatens to smother.

Silver Strings of Mental Health

Hellhole

Glenside, 1987

I am unwell
but I have hope.
I still like
to be touched
and to dream
of healing hands –
I do not have enough
of this human medicine.

They cry
out loud.
For God's sake
don't feed it,
don't ignore it,
just stroke it
and be kind.

Nurturing the Taproot

I am happy now
learning all the time.
I think I am content.
I think I know it all.

Then whispers of indifference
tiptoe through my brain.
Shadows of doubts
make me think I'm going insane.

Impressions
continually changing.
My core remains
undisturbed.

Just Resorts

Glenside is not so bad.
Every now and then
people need to be forced
to rest, to eat well
and take fresh air
and sunshine.

A psychiatric institution
is often
a poor man's holiday
a place of safety
and support
a resort without
the beach.

Heaven in Hell

There's lots of heaven in hell
and I like it this way.
Mental health sufferers
or people with vices
are not evil.
We feel more
in our brief time
here with the devil.

Look up
savour the blue
and the happy times;
live slowly and know
that the bad years
are irrelevant
and good years beckon.
So, smokers, gamblers,
drinkers, thinkers,
drug addicts, pill-afflicted,
look up, savour
being you.

Eye of the Storm

I am well
within my prison
of sickness.
Running
with the human race,
I set my own pace.
I was born different
I had to fight
but I am well
within the prison cell
of my sickness.

I Must Walk in a Straight Line

Man,
I am beginning
to feel
fine again.
I know
I must walk
in a straight
line again.
I am starting
to shine again.
I have not blown
my life yet.
My line,
my life
is cruising,
yes, I have my bruising
but letting go now
I no longer
fear the foul
but a warm embrace
and the fresh kiss
of each new day.

Love's Healing Grace

Love

Love.
Love?
Love!
A stepping stone
to heaven
above.

Forget Being a Princess

Princesses
are like queen ants
kept hidden
jealously guarded
used to procreate.

And remember,
bull ants
eat their own.

Living on the Line

for L W B

I live
on
the poverty line
a thin line
yet I feel
like a queen
nothing fancy
but
I have
love
hope
faith
and my own
good grace.

Barnacles

No man
no cries
no goodbyes.
Men are coral
or painful
barnacles
stuck to
the even keel
of my past.

Relationship Breakdown

I am so confused.
My man says he can't win.
We are at odds
two odd sods –
Who knows how
we ever communicated?
Nothing new.
Same old thing.
It's hard to grasp
that love won't last.
Oops, where's my foot?
In my mouth;
another sweet flower
turned sour.

Role Play

1.

OK, women,
we have proven our point.
We are as equal as we can be
to man. We can do what we can,
sometimes better, sometimes worse.
What have we proved?
Maybe a lot.
Maybe a little.
but how great it is to try.
Been there, done that.
Let's stop today
and settle things once
and for all…
man is not good
without woman…
and hell,
women is not good
without man.

2.

OK, men,
off your pedestals.
Mentally we're your equal,
functionally your match.
We have brought you
down to learn
softened your hearts
lessened your load.
But don't become too weak,
we still need your strength.
And appreciate us.
No, take your lead
and we will support
and guide you.
But don't ever
take us for granted.
Love's flame is not easy
to rekindle.

3.

We all know
as hydrogen molecules
we are bonded together.
Inseparable.
We need each other.
We are of the same strength
a balance, a strain.
But one can't do without
the weight of the other.
Accept. Thrust into the world
a newly drawn line.
Let men be men
women be women
in love.

Life on Earth

Fruit and Vegetables

Fruit and veg
are the essence
of my life…
their succulent insides
their taste, their feel
their smell of life.

Drive me wild
O aubergine
lead me O lychee,
like an innocent child
with a thirsty lust
for some neighbour's
forbidden fruit.

The sweet juice
 the smooth skin
  the seeds
   the flesh.

This Life…

so complex
if you attempt to unravel
the precision-made puzzle
a challenge will unfold.

The system
is simple
if only you appreciated
the simple things.
The miracle of a clear glass window
opening, of a faucet spouting water.

Acting on Life's Big Stage

Odd people
pulling faces
trying hard
to act the part.

I am acting too.
in multiple roles.
Without even trying.

The art is
quietly laughing
to myself

on that big, strange stage
of illusions.

Ticking

Time is the hunter
we are its prey.
Light switch on
then off so soon.
I have lived long
in the great spirit land
at the mercy of
time's hand.
I fought hard
but now
I let it flow
and imagine
like John Lennon
times of peace
ticking over one day.
And when the hunter's big hand comes
we bend over
and kiss our own
sweet selves
goodbye.

Freedom's Key

Let Me be Free to be Me

I love to wander through the streets,
not knowing which people I'll meet.
I just have to get out of my cage
for a little while.
I need to see other people
and, if I'm lucky, catch a smile.
I order a cappuccino
read my magazine
and admire the tiny bunch of flowers
I have purchased.
The silence in their beauty
makes me feel alive.
Small luxuries
break the monotony.

Keep Looking

What have we lost?
What have we found?
Have we found our true selves;
our roots?
Or are we all caught –
jesters and wise owls
kings and queens
caught within our own plays?

We must not let
the whirlwinds of our minds
consume us.
If we look, learn and seek,
yesterday is history
tomorrow a mystery.
Our date with destiny
hiding, smiling
just around the corner.

Hard to be Alone and Happy

It is just as hard to be alone and happy
as it is to be together and happy.

The price you pay to be free
is as high as it is to be committed.

One is as confusing as the other –
so you take your path, choose your road

carefully.

Free?

In my little cage
I sit
wondering…
Oh wherefore art thou key,
oh key
to set my little heart
and soul free?

But as I wait
and as I watch
from the security
of my cage,
I can see
a shocking sight…

the door is open
it has always been so
and it's up to me
to set myself free.

I Need Some Polish

Wrack my brain.
Whip my soul.
I am feeling like
a bowl of old
sour cream –
full of mouldy dreams
and bacteria.

Am I redundant?
Or just in need of some polish
a little gleam
because my exterior
coat has faded.

I push myself
into gear
stop feeling
like a smear
on the window
of life.

I'm ready to shine.
Come on, girl,
brighten up!

The Human Soup

I am not a good enough vegetable
for certain people's soup.
So I will be a Melba toast
with sour cream, salmon
and caviar on top.

I thank my friends and my daughter
that my brew is always true.
Tears may fall in
and strangers stir it up
but I'd rather be me
than many other monkeys
swimming in the human soup.

About the Author

At the age of seventeen, I travelled the United States and Canada by bus for four months, before becoming a bank officer for three years, winning Miss Bank of SA Bathing Beauty Contest, the prize being a return trip to Perth, Western Australia. I also played in the Under 16, Under 18 and Under 20 state basketball teams, and was awarded a basketball scholarship at the Australian Institute of Sport. I played for Australia against Japan and Korea in Asia.

At the age of twenty, I left the bank and ran away with a circus. We travelled Australia and I sold fluffy toys and fruit salad. I then landed a job on a fishing boat as a deckhand with a German man and his family. We worked in the Bass Strait around the Furneaux group of islands. I love the sea immensely. It was a great source of inspiration to me. We explored islands, ate lobster and worked very hard.

Then I embarked on a brief modelling career. My first assignment was for Sussan, a national clothing company. Next I coached and played basketball in Tasmania. I enjoyed many rural activities, including cattle mustering, horse riding, four-wheel driving and bushwalking. I loved living in the country.

At the age of twenty, I wrote my first poetry collection, *Impressions of a Young Traveller*, and two years later I wrote a biography about an Australian adventurer. I have also worked as a gym manageress and aerobics instructor, and in waitressing, public relations and promotions, and was a company manager and band manager. I have had about twenty different jobs in my life because I love variety.

I married an Australian pianist and had a beautiful daughter,

Lucy. In 1987 I suffered an illness, and while recovering I volunteered for the Red Cross, Royal Society for the Blind, Salvation Army and a Women's Community Centre. Currently I am working on a novel.

Sue Amanda Carter

www.ingramcontent.com/pod-product-compliance
Lightning Source LLC
Chambersburg PA
CBHW062152100526
44589CB00014B/1796